# SERVING TO THE TOP

## DR. ROBIN LOCOCO

PUBLISHED BY Live To Produce Publishing Group |Productive
Business Civility

# Table of Contents

# Endorsements

Dr. Robin Lococo is in a class by herself, she is a woman of action. When you look at her body of work, well over 20 years of serving humanity, you see a leader at the forefront of change. This book regarding service should be on every bookshelf in the world.

Dr. Lococo is truly an example of how you can serve your way to the top. I have watched her serve in Africa, the Middle East, Latin America, and the United States of America, and every single person, no matter their plight in life, got her top service with no partiality. I have watched this firsthand for over 25 years. She has served her way to the Top 20 Women of the Year Congressional Award from congressman Danny K. Davis from Illinois. Then one year later she received a Presidential Lifetime Achievement award from the United States of America. I have watched no one in the world receive these kinds of awards that have never touched the microphone on an international stage. These awards have come from total service and service only, this is truly a book you will want to read from the Mother of Global Service.

Thank you for your unconditional years of service.

Amb. Clyde Rivers

It is an absolute pleasure to know and to work with Dr. Robin Lococo. She is an excellent leader with a heart of gold. Robin is a true giant who is changing the lives of Challenged Champions and Heroes worldwide. Dr. Lococo is fulfilling her dreams and assists others in making their dreams come true.

Prof. Dr. Vernet A. Joseph

Founder of Productive Business Civility.

Dr. Robin Mosier Lococo is a person every community should want to have, because her commitment to bring Justice and Civility to the community is Paramount. She started, and has maintained beautifully, a "Grassroots" organization that brings honor and awareness to individuals with physical challenges in our society today, in various areas. Robin is a "Visionary and Trendsetter" and has a unique perspective, which makes her a "Valuable Asset" to whatever she's involved in. She is recognized as a subject matter expert in this area. She is highly decorated by various notable organizations globally because of the knowledge she possesses. It's an Honor & Privilege for me to tell the reader of this book about my amazing friend Dr. Robin Mosier Lococo.

Dr. Anthony "Coach Tony" Branch

iChange Nations World Civility Ambassador

Author & Motivational Speaker, and Youth Activist

# *Preface*

The thought of writing this book on selfless service "Serving to the Top" all started as I received the Top 20 Women of the World Woman's Day Award, a Congressional Award given by Danny K. Davis, a congressman from Chicago Illinois. This award was given for my International service and humanitarian work with my organization called Challenged Champions and Heroes and my humanitarian work in Africa and around the world. I have also recently received a Presidential Award for my humanitarian service. This award was given and signed by President Donald Trump in recognition of over 4,000 service hours to humanity. I never really thought about my service being recognized the way it has been, it is just something I have always done naturally; I never asked for this to happen and was totally shocked when it did. I have always been the one that has been happy serving in the background, not looking to be the one recognized upfront or in the limelight in any way. For 25 years now I have served Dr. Rivers in administration, or in whatever office was needed at the time. Anyone that knows Dr. Rivers and the life he has led is amazed at how many people he has been able to help throughout the world. In this book I will share more about our stories of how we have worked together throughout the years serving others and building a culture of honor throughout the world.

It is my hope that this book will be a book of encouragement and strength and hope to all those that read it.

*Believe*

ALL THINGS ARE POSSIBLE IF YOU BELIEVE
–Mark 9:23

# References

*All scripture references and Bible stories were taken from the King James Version.

For more information on iChange Nations or Challenged Champions and Heroes please contact:

Dr. Robin A. Lococo at:

Robin.challengedchampions@gmail.com

https://www.challengedchampionsandheros.com/

# Introduction

Throughout my life I have matured from a quiet and shy person to a leader that started my own organization and a leader that is overseeing and leading thousands. I have overcome what people said I could not do in life. I have even completed my education later in life with earned Doctorate degrees in Christian Counseling from United Graduate College and Seminary International and a Doctorate in Society and Humans Rights from Latin University of Theology. While completing my education I was *serving others* at the same time through working in the administration of each of these schools. I am now facilitating and administrating education models in over 80 countries. I am also the general overseer of a ministry accreditation program that equips ministries with accreditations and ordinations and endorses schools all over the world. I have traveled all over the United States and internationally to Uganda, Kenya, Ivory Coast, Nigeria, Dubai, Guyana, Guatemala, and London, so far. This is just the beginning of my incredible journey. My life has been exciting, to say the least, living the Golden Rule and doing my part to make the world a better place. "Serving to the Top" has become a reality for me and I want you to know that if it can happen for me it can happen for you!

# Reaching the
## unreachable

Mark 2:13-17

As I began to think about writing this book, I wanted to make it a think book to encourage you, the reader, to really look at your own philosophy of serving. So, when you see THINK BOOK take a moment to consider the question and write down your answer.

Before you begin reading, *at this present time* please answer the following question:

THINK BOOK 💡 What does serving look like to you at this moment?

_____

_____

_____

_____

_____

_____

_____

# Chapter 1

## The Step Up

## (Small Beginnings)

My journey around the world, 25 years of service with Dr. Rivers, and, of course, my relationship with God has taught me many things. I am not the person I was early on in life. Looking back on my life it's hard to find or pinpoint just one moment; there have been many moments or a series of events that helped make me who I've become, building the foundation of passion that I have today to help people.

How I was raised, the people I know, each event of my life, all helped to shape and mold me into who I am today. I would like to start not with the "one" defining moment in my life that made me who I am today, but the *Lifestyle* I have lived. I want to encourage you to not disregard the small beginnings or the small steps in life. Even your setbacks play an important role in life. I hope in reading this book all will be inspired.

I was born a fighter; life tried to take me out early, but it did not succeed. I was born in 1961 and my mother was 46 years old, well past her prime childbearing years, and not in the best of health, she both smoked and drank, but she was determined to have a baby girl. (My older sister Debra died of Cerebral Palsy at age three). I was born 2 ½ months premature and my life began with me fighting to survive. Born a preemie is defined as a baby that is under 1 3/4 pounds and is generally born before 26 weeks gestation, but most people prefer to loosen this term up to include any baby under 3 pounds or under 29 weeks gestation. Back in 1961, babies that were born that early usually did not survive because we did not have the medical technology that we have today.

After many months of fighting to survive and with a will that would not quit, I was strong enough to go home at a victorious, whopping 5 pounds. From birth to age 11 my life was good. I thrived and had a pretty good life, until my mother died abruptly, at the young age of 56, from a heart attack brought on by cirrhosis of the liver. I was just a young 11-year-old girl and my world shattered. For whatever his reasons, and I truly still don't know why to this day, my father sent me off to live at my friend's house after my mother's death. "While he got himself together," I guess. I was left feeling alone and abandoned once again. I stayed with my friend and their family for over a year. I was suddenly in a strange city, with strange people; in fact, a whole new culture of people, going from suburban small-town Chardon to the urban rough city of Warren, Ohio. Feeling scared and alone it was all quite a shock; I believe this was what caused me to be a very quiet and shy person growing up. I quietly watched and learned about the world around me. Now being the minority myself, living in Warren, Ohio, I learned to love all races, I learned to embrace all differences in people – personalities and ways of living; even now, there is not a prejudiced bone in my body.

Although I loved school, my school days were also difficult. Because of my size, I was always looked at differently;

sometimes teased and sometimes babied. There was always someone there to try to help me or try to comfort me, or to tell me I couldn't do it. "Here, let me help you" was always ringing in my ears. Even as I took my first step to get on the school bus, on the first day of kindergarten, I needed help; although, that time I truly needed the help, because I physically could not reach the step. At age 6, I was far smaller than everyone else my age. Even then, I knew I was different somehow. Knowing this, even at this early age created a new fight, and determination within me.

I have always had a passion to help people. In high school I went through a course called DHO, Diversified Health Occupations, a vocational program that covers all medical-related fields. I loved working with the Special Needs groups. I first wanted to work in the area of physical therapy with children, but my teacher quickly shattered that dream when she said I could not physically handle the job; lifting patients would be an impossibility for me.

Twenty years later I faced another setback. I went to school to be a school bus driver; this time I asked at the start, "Do you think I will have any problems in applying for this job?" "Not at all," they replied. I completed the eight-week course with flying colors at the top of the class, with the highest scores and perfect attendance. I went on to do the behind the wheel test at the bus yard to be hired for a driver. Before I even got to back up the bus, the instructor stopped me. "You came up off the seat a little when you pushed in the clutch, we can't have that; that is a safety issue," she said. "I was told at the beginning of the course you would work with me with blocks or pillows if necessary, or I'm perfectly able to drive the smaller buses," I said. "I'm sorry, we need someone to be able to drive ALL the buses; we cannot help you with blocks or pillows." Oh no, not again, I thought.

That made me even more determined to be strong and win at whatever I did. Nobody was going to tell me I couldn't do it. Through it all, the constant obstacles, teasing, and putdowns about my height, I managed to overcome and even thrive in life. I have learned over the years that obstacles are no problem. Even though I have had many obstacles and I come from a small town, I want you to know big dreams can still happen and be rewarded.

This book will show you through my own life that anybody can serve and show love to another human being if we can just look beyond the outside, look beyond our differences for we are really all the same on the inside.

Part of my philosophy in life is to live The Golden Rule: "Do unto others as you have them do unto you." This motto is alive and well in my heart. Because I know what it's like to be treated unfairly or differently. I've learned not to compare myself to others by asking why I am different, but to take pride in the fact that I AM different and special, and there is no one like me! There is a quote by TD Jakes that says, "Your flaws make you unique, your uniqueness makes you valuable." So, embrace your differences. It's what makes you *uniquely* you.

Embracing my own differences has given me a passion for fighting for the underdog or those that are different in some way. I remember an incident where I was hanging out with some friends after school, and they were teasing and mocking a mentally handicapped person we saw earlier at the store. Calling him "Spedly" short for Special Education, I guess. At that point I wondered why they were my friends; how could they be so mean to another person. Well, I went ballistic! Going off on them with some not so choice words. This incident proved to be the beginning of my fighting and/or standing up for the underdog or those that are different in some way.

As for myself – concerning my size, don't misunderstand my small statue as weakness. I have passion just like anyone else. Strength is in the spirit of the person and passion comes from the heart. Let me tell you strength does not always have anything to do with size or the outward appearances. If there's something that you excel at or have a talent at, focus on that. Keep working hard at your talent and people will recognize you for that and not your height or whatever your difference may be.

I now honor who I am and can honor others who are different, who are great, and are making a difference in the world!

Through my organization called Challenged Champions and Heroes, I bring honor and recognition to the Differently Abled and their Caregivers.

There is no greater disability in society, than the inability to see a person as more. Robert M. Hansel

# Chapter 2

## Why Not You?

God seeks and values the gifts we bring Him, gifts of praise, thanksgiving, service, and material offerings. But the greatest gift acceptable to God is in the measure to which the one who offers it is in fellowship with Him in character and conduct; and the greatest test of this is in our relationships and conduct with our fellow man. How do we interact with our family, neighbors, our community, and the rest of the world? Look at the crime rates today in America, school shootings, drug addiction, mental health issues, and homelessness to name just a few. There are endless opportunities to find an area to be of help. Crime rates in America as reported in 2017 according to Wikipedia: violent crimes were 5.3 for homicides, 41.7 for rape, 98.0 for robberies, and 248.9 for aggravated assaults for a total of 382.9 crimes per 100,000 people; the estimated total population at the time was 325,719,178. These are staggering numbers.

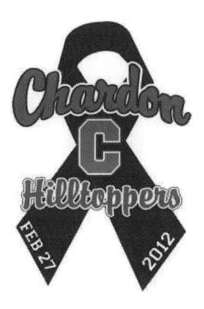

School shootings have become commonplace in America. On February 27, 2012, exactly 8 years prior to the time I am now writing this book, a shooting took place at *MY HIGH SCHOOL*, Chardon High in Chardon, Ohio. That shooting resulted in the deaths of three male student victims within two days of the incident. Witnesses said that the shooter had a personal rivalry with one of the victims. Two other wounded students were hospitalized, one of whom sustained several serious injuries that have resulted in permanent paralysis. The fifth student suffered a minor injury, and the sixth a superficial wound. If these issues can hit so close to home for me, they can for you also. *Humanity needs you.* Today in our society, unfortunately, most people are only concerned about three people: Me, Myself, and I. It's still all about self. It's a selfish world out there. You must look really close to see people doing good for another. I am guilty of this, also; I have neighbors that have lived across the street from me for two years and I barely talk to them. Just an occasional hello or wave, they have three children and I couldn't tell you their names. It is sad but all too true. Getting to know people who live nearby creates a sense of belonging and shared identity in our local area. It helps to strengthen connections in the wider communities and contributes to a healthier community overall for everyone.

Today in America and around the world we are experiencing the Coronavirus outbreak or Covid19. Since President Trump announced it to be a pandemic everyone has gone crazy! People are in a panic. Because most are only thinking about themselves, they are stockpiling, and hoarding, buying everything up in the stores. Fear breeds greed and every evil work, it also produces the let's save ourselves mentality. This is happening even more now because of our society is already stuck in the me, myself and I mindset. I witnessed a woman clear out the whole section of Kraft boxed Macaroni and Cheese with one swoop of her arm. Is it necessary to buy 75 boxes at one time? We have also witnessed a man buy $500 worth of canned goods. This has led the grocery stores to have a no return policy and set limits on purchases. Amazon and eBay stopped people from selling these items online.

When will humanity really "see" what is happening in the times we are living in? How much we need the value in seeing beyond one's self? The value in reaching out to someone with a helping hand. We all need a helping hand at one time or another. Why wait till it is needed or we are in a crisis to extend a hand to someone else? Do it just because you can. Just because showing love to another human being is the right thing to do. Real and true perception is seeing what humanity can do for one another. It takes practice but once one "sees" it can become a whole new world. Sight is common but true vision is rare. Seeing beyond one's self, to having a vision into the future to help others and make a lasting *manifesting* change is what the world needs from all of us.

Concerning our conduct to our fellowman, our ethical behavior toward one another should be affectively grounded in compassion, creating new nurturing and social bonds with others.

THINK BOOK 💡 When you see people in need how do you respond?

_____

_____

_____

_____

_____

_____

_____

_____

In today's times it's hard to know how to respond. Have you been driving along and see people standing on the street corner asking for money or food? My heart is to help them, but I know most of the time they are running a scam. How do we recognize the difference? How do we keep our hearts pure to help others when we see this happening through others?

When it comes to giving, there are three types of people overall: The first are already actively prosocial; they will continue to be during this crisis. The second focus more on themselves, while caring little what happens to others. In today's unprecedented circumstances, however, even they would tend to act prosocially. This comes back to the idea of generalized reciprocity, plus slowing the spread of the virus to protect themselves. The final group is competitive; they care how they are doing in comparison to others and want to come out on top. However, there are situations when this competitive person will set aside their competitive urge because if they don't set aside their competitive side, they will be opening themselves up to a lot of social scorn (Watson, Galadrel) Washington Post.

One way of helping is not only by serving or giving to another but to empower them. The old saying, "Give a man a fish, and you feed him for a day. Teach a man to fish, and you feed him for a lifetime," focuses on the idea that long term benefits are more useful than the short-term benefits. The same is so with serving. As others see you serving with the right heart it is empowering. It gives them the opportunity and ability to learn from your example. Showing that you truly care and are present in the moment with them. Taking your time and attention to be with them, looking them in the eyes as you are speaking to each other.

As I discuss more about the traits of a servant and the examples, I have set forth in *my life* you can see just how empowering serving others can be. With every new work we took on we touched more and more lives. With each person we touched, they touched and empowered others. Jesus started his ministry with twelve disciples and served the multitudes. How much more can we do? Who are you called to serve?

Jesus was a *servant of God,* and a *servant of man. Servant* is mentioned 491 times in the Bible. So why is showing love and compassion to another human being through servanthood so important?

The Bible states: It is an honor and a privilege to serve others and *obey the words of your father*; as a matter of fact, it is considered a "key of life" as stated in this Bible verse. Wisdom is a key to life for those who find it (Proverbs 4:22).

"Withhold not good from them to whom it is due, when it is in the power of your hand to do it. Say not unto your neighbor, Go, and come again, and tomorrow I will give... (Proverb 3:27-28).

You see life's rewards are in direct proportion to the lives of others we serve. Not only does it change the mindset of the me, myself, and I, it provides other benefits we will discuss later in this book.

God is so eager to see his people blessed that he provided a way for us to succeed even when humanity occasionally falls short. God has made a fail-safe way for us to enter his fullness in life, and it is called grace. Grace is the main ingredient that allows us to succeed even when we fall short. Do your best to keep your grace account toward others full. Oh, yes, this reminds me of another story, in Uganda. We have drivers that take us all around the city, and on this day, we noticed that the gas tank was on empty. We suggested that we stop to get gas and our driver replied "E" is not for empty, it means "Enough." So, it is with our grace account with God, it will never run empty.

# Chapter 3

## Fundamentals of Serving

*Everyone can be great, because
everybody can serve.*

## Dr. Martin Luther King, Jr.

❧

What does it mean to become a selfless servant? Selfless is defined as having little or no concern for oneself, especially regarding fame or position. A servant is a person in the service of another.

Mark 10:45 states that Jesus came to serve not to be served. A servant is always giving of oneself to minister to others and to do whatever it takes to accomplish what is best for another.

Phil.1:4 states that we are to be *concerned for others*; Paul prayed daily for others. How often do you go out of the way to help others if there is nothing in it for you? Every Christian is gifted for service and with the gift of operations is where we find the Greek word energema, from which we get our English word energy. So spiritual gifts are also energizing. It is likely that this word emphasizes the divine energy enabling us to perform the service. Peter has this very idea in mind when he says to minister or serve with the ability or strength which God gives (I Peter 4:11). God's gifts in us give us the ability to perform service in His strength. So, all of us can serve. From praying in the Upper Room – yes, prayer is service – to the record of Paul's "proclaiming the Kingdom of God and teaching about the Lord Jesus Christ with all boldness and without hindrance" (Acts 28:31) from prison, these early Spirit-filled Christians went everywhere in the *service* of their risen Lord. We can also be a service to other believers to help make their mission easier.

An example of this in the Old Testament would be as Joshua was to Moses or Elisha was to Elijah. Joshua was eventually promoted to a leader of all Israel and Elisha went on to receive a double portion of the anointing that Elijah had, performing even more miracles than his mentor. So, as you can see with the story of Elisha and Elijah, God rewards those who serve others. Therefore, I believe the same has happened for me, in all my years of service with Dr. Rivers and all the different ministries I have worked with I have also received a double portion. You don't have to be a believer to serve and have compassion for others. God has already put that gift in everyone. He has created us in his image and likeness. We as human beings were created to serve and have compassion for others. So, whether you are a believer or not, all can serve. Just like the body has a fight or flight mechanism when the body senses danger, the brain also has a compassion response-built in. Compassion is deeply rooted in our human nature; it has a biological basis in our brain and bodies.

Our communities are only as healthy as our conceptions of human nature. It has long been assumed that selfishness, greed, and competitiveness lie at the core of our human behavior and are the products of our society. These assumptions have guided most realms of life, from policymaking to how the media portrays people on the news. If all we see on the news is bad, which is what we are seeing now with this pandemic, that is the reality most people will believe. Feeling compassion for another is one thing but acting on it is another. Research shows when we encounter people in need or in distress, we put ourselves in their position and imagine what their experience is like, this is a very positive thing. By looking at another person's perspective we can then form our own judgments, this is when our compassion switch is turned on and we can feel empathy and concern for others which in turn motivates us to address other people's needs, sometimes at the expense of our own.

Looking at your own life: what area might you be called to be a service in? Most people look at their profession as their service to humanity. A job is just a job if you don't enjoy it. It provides a way to pay the bills and provide for your family. There are many jobs that provide services to another: waitresses serve their customers; doctors and nurses serve their patients; attorneys are there to serve their clients. But let's look beyond it being just a job.

In my life I became a caregiver to my husband for two years. This is not something I did because I enjoyed it, but it was needed at the time. I was thrust into a caregiver position when my husband had his third stroke and was unable to care for himself anymore. At this time, we had been separated for many years and he was living by himself. I discovered later that I did not necessarily dislike this work. Since I was already being a caregiver, to my husband, I registered and began working as a caregiver through IHSS for the county of San Bernardino. I started this job, as I said earlier, just to make a little extra money, but it turned out I really started to like it. I started working for a sweet lady that was 79 years old. She just needed someone to help with light cooking, cleaning, laundry, and taking her to Dr. appointments and running errands. Although I didn't work for her long, because of her declining health, we became good friends. She stated many times I was the best caregiver she had had. Now, I can look back at this experience and have fond memories of how in the last year of her life *I made a difference* in her life. We enjoyed many laughs together; I took her out for a special birthday celebration and to her favorite restaurants, as much as I could, when she was feeling up to it, of course. She was not able to do much on her low income, so it was a blessing for me to be able to do that for her. I did as many things as I could to make that time of her life special. I now am taking care of her little dog for her since her passing and I think about her all the time.

My point here is to not be afraid to step out and try new things, you might find out you like it. Look to interact with people you have never met before and try new activities around your neighborhood. What started as a neighborhood project can grow into helping the community, city, state, and maybe even worldwide as it did for me. You will find that you usually don't have to look too far to find someone in need. The Bible states: in *all things* that we do, and by working hard we must *always look* to help those that need help and remember the words of the Lord Jesus, "It is more blessed to give than to receive" (paraphrase of Acts 20:35). I encourage you to step out and try something new, you just might enjoy it.

Look at your life in practical theory, right now:

THINK BOOK 💡 How could you be the answer to someone else's problem?

_____

_____

_____

_____

_____

# Chapter 4

## The Heart of The Servant

In this chapter I'll go over some important personality traits of a servant. In some examples I'll use my serving as it pertains to my gift of Administration and how it is applied.

A servant *loves and is compassionate*. All you need is love, and love is all others need. Love gives to others. Matthew 25:45, "He will reply, 'I tell you the truth, whatever you do for one of the least of these, you do for me.'" Showing love to others will always come back to you. A servant loves doing for others sometimes to the exclusion of meeting their own personal needs. John 15:9-17, "As the Father has loved me, so have I loved you. Now remain in my love, just as I have kept my Father's commands and remain in his love. My command is this: Love each other as I have first loved you. Greater love has no man but to lay his life down for another. You did not choose me, but I chose YOU and appointed you so that you might go and bear fruit, fruit that will last, and so whatever you ask in my name the Father will give you. This is my command: Love each other." The word love appears nine times in these verses. Jesus tells us what it means to love. He tells us how transformative both love in our relationship with Christ and with others can be. We are called to love one another, just as Christ first loved us. How many people do you know that are willing to give up their life for you? Love can be learned and the best way to teach others is by first being a good example.

The servant not only has love but also a compassion that moves them to action on behalf of those in need. Compassion is not simply caring about others, but such a radical caring that we have no choice but to make sacrifices for others. Those with the gift of compassion rarely ask, "Should I help," but instead focus on how to help. In administration, a person of compassion would always look to find a better way of doing things for the betterment of the body. Compassion also makes us fundamentally aware of the Christ in us and gives us our desire to care for all of God's creatures and creation. I encourage you to choose a life serving others and watch the ripple effect that unlocks the compassion in others. When someone shows you compassion look for ways you can pay it forward. Servants look for ways to do for others both within and beyond the congregation and community. A servant serves where needed giving up their free time whether it's changing a tire or changing a diaper. A servant serves (or not) as God directs – unbelief that God "is working" on our behalf causes us to move in our own strength and usually causes us to move too fast or in the wrong direction. Allow God to lead you. Do what you can, when you can, as an opportunity arises. If you see a need, be a seed. Be available to serve always.

Servants do not choose to serve but serve from a sense of identity and calling. Gifted servants are less likely to feel put-upon or taken advantage of but see each opportunity to do for others as an opportunity to be true to themselves. Not all are *gifted,* but all can serve. Those that don't have the gift of a servant can overextend themselves very quickly. They will become frustrated that people do not react the way they had hoped for when they do an act of kindness to another. I will cover this more in a later chapter.

Let your actions speak louder than words, let not your words run ahead of your hands and feet. What do I mean by this statement? A true servant leader is driven by actions that earn respect and not just an impressive title. A servant serves freely not looking for what is in it for them. They are not interested only in beauty, brawn, bucks, power, prestige, or the highest position. Over the years, I have seen many church leaders run straight to the Pastor seeking to be up front as a group leader or to preach up front. Most are only there to serve themselves, looking to fill their own desires not necessarily to serve the people. Their true heart shines through very quickly as to why they are there. As a rule, we have always made our gifted leaders at our church sit down and wait for 6 months and learn before being put into a leadership position. True serving means serving with a clean heart with no hidden motives. I have seen this also works well for people that are asking for money or free handouts. Out of a good heart you may want to help them out right away by giving them money. But sometimes it is good to have the person asking for money come to stay during the service or come back to the following service to help them. This will show the true intentions of their heart also. If they just want money for alcohol or drugs they will usually not come back. If their heart is sincere and they really are looking for help they will stay and even come back. We have now looked at love and compassion and how a servant responds to others. Let's look at a few other traits of a servant.

A servant *gives*; giving is the deep commitment to provide whatever resources are needed to support God's will and plan. In addition to radical generosity, those who possess the gift of giving have the uncanny ability to discover and channel new sources of money, time, and energy to needs. Money management skills grant writing abilities, and the easy knack of asking for donations and cultivating donors are among the common skills of givers. There is a quote by Anne Frank that I love that states: "No one has ever become poor by giving."

A servant *helps*; helping is a gift of support and behind-the-scenes effort that makes groups, families, and congregations more effective. Not everyone is gifted to lead, but many are gifted to follow and handle the tasks that are so essential;

although, this is less glamorous, it is proven to be more rewarding. Helpers love to serve others, support others, and assist others in the important work of ministry and missions. Tireless in their willingness to serve, helpers are less interested in receiving thanks and recognition than in doing good, valuable work.

Servants need to have *patience*; one of the biggest hindrances in serving is patience. People are easily distracted and go from one thing to another never completing the task at hand. Servants need to have patience; it is a key trait just like love and compassion is. Others are watching how you may handle the situation at hand. You might be the first and only light that they will see. If you feel yourself losing it, it might be time to take a step back for a moment. We will discuss this more in Chapter 7 Knowing your Limits.

A servant is humble; they never think they are better than anyone else, a humble heart recognizes that when pointing out someone else's fault you have 4 more fingers pointing back at you.

A servant has discernment; discernment is a gift of deep intuition and insight. Discerning people can separate truth from fiction and know at a natural level when people are being honest. Deeply sensitive and "tuned in," those with the gift of discernment are open to feelings. In the area of administration, new ideas and intuition come as valid and credible information.

A servant is effective, not just busy. A servant prepares, with gratitude and love; we train by doing, learning to be the most effective servant possible. Even when you don't know what you're doing, it is always an opportunity to learn.

A servant is longsuffering. A servant expects to suffer as Jesus's light shines through us. People who love darkness (John 3:19) will become convicted and uncomfortable in the light of his glory and will hate and ridicule those who are trying to serve them.

A servant perseveres; the work we've been given is long and tiring, receives little thanks or recognition, and may seem to count for little while it's being done. Continuing in such work is a challenge none of us is up to on our own. Love overcomes all things.

A servant is an influencer serving without expectation: The greatest gift from God is the ability to influence others in a positive way by your actions.

Greatness is not found in a title, a salary, or a worldly position of influence. True and eternal greatness is spiritual influence, the only influence that is eternal, it can only be found in servanthood – intentionally and willingly meeting the needs of others in the power of the Holy Spirit, without looking for recognition from people, and leaving the results to God.

# Chapter 5

## Loyalty Over Little

Miracle Faith Church was started in 1994 by Pastor Clyde Rivers. The name itself says a lot because we live by *miracle faith* every day. At the start of the church, even Pastor Clyde didn't have a car; the Pastor had to call on his church members to get a ride to church, that's not something you hear every day. The church began at a church member's private home with a handful of members. We quickly outgrew the house and needed a bigger space. Along came another miracle – one of our members worked for the city and fought for us to rent space at a school facility. This was frowned upon at the time because they were trying to separate church from state and not allowing churches to rent public city buildings. This lady fought every month to keep us in that building for Wednesday and Sunday services. The church grew to about 200 members and that was about the time that I started going to Miracle Faith Church. My first Sunday was Easter Sunday 1996 and I've been there ever since. Going to church was not always voluntary for me. My husband was attending the church before me, he got me to go because Miracle Faith Church was starting a softball team and, on this weekend, they had a game. Being the sports fan that I am, I decided to go check it out, and I ran across somebody that I worked with who also attended there. God works things out perfectly – he knew what would grab my attention. Well, things started to move fast after that. I began doing administrative work for the church after six months in attendance. I've now been there 25 years and throughout the years have helped people in many ways.

Along with the administration of the church, I administrated three Miracle Faith Church Bible study training centers. I have also worked in conjunction with community-based feeding programs in the high desert feeding the homeless. I work closely with the city of Victorville scheduling the invocations.

I assisted the high desert event coordinator for the March of Jesus in 1999. Worked closely with the music coordinator for the High Desert Gospel Festival in 1998. Worked in conjunction with Hope Chest, a food and clothing distribution ministry, for the people of the high desert in 2001. Assisted in establishing the Jesus Fan Club at Silverado High School in 2001. Helped establish and coordinate a convalescent home outreach ministry to elderly residents. Outreach members went room to room visiting and praying for patients as well as provided a weekly church service.

Assisted in the founding and establishing of Warriors for Christ a ministry dedicated to youth in 1997; we provided citywide youth rallies that included hip-hop and rock concerts and the preaching of the word of God. All this time I looked only to serve others, although I considered this my job it never felt like work to me. There is a saying: "If you find your passion, you will never *work* a day in your life." We have looked to help others so much within the High Desert Communities that we would often give the offerings back to the church that invited us in to minister to the people.

Over the years I have heard comments such as "Do you do everything Clyde tells you? Why don't you get a real job? How do you live like that?" Meaning with no guarantee of a salary. I have lived the life of faith since 2002, I have learned the obedience of faith is using what you have, and God will provide the rest. I know God will give me what I need when I need it. Use what you have not what you don't.

Every year life just gets bigger and better. It's something I can't explain or understand this thing called faith, but I can see the effects of believing and I know in my heart this is what God wants me to be doing, so I stepped forward, not wavering in my faith.

Every day fighting the battles that you hear in your mind like, "I don't feel like I'm doing anything. Why don't I just quit?" When you hear these thoughts let me tell you, keep going and keep walking, this is a clear indication that God is with you, and you're on the right track.

Inch by inch we win, keep moving. It takes commitment and focus when you are feeling like you're not doing enough. Seemingly small random acts of kindness lead to accumulated goodness.

The gift of faith is more than just the belief in Jesus Christ. It is an abiding foundation of confidence that God works all things together for good, that all things are possible, and that the people of God can rise above any obstacle. In the gift of Administration, faith is very necessary in meeting deadlines and completing unexpected tasks. Faith is the bedrock upon which we build lives, congregations, and communities. People with the gift of faith hold fast to the deep conviction that no matter what we see with our eyes, we can trust the promises and plan of God. Let me share some more of the stories of how God has worked in my life. I have spoken about how I have served others in my immediate community let's expand statewide.

I have assisted in the established monthly youth rallies in Lancaster, California; assisted in the establishing of prophetic music concerts at Venice Beach and Venice Foursquare Church; assisted in the establishment of the prophetic music concerts at the 3rd St. Promenade in Santa Monica California;

and administrated the Special Ops network, which networks ministries in order to provide training and support for the various ministries statewide. I worked with Henry Mena and Teen Blaze youth churches and was appointed overseer of administration for Latin University of Theology English extensions.

We were faithful to drive every Tuesday night to Lancaster to be a part of a good Pastor friend's Tuesday night Bible studies. We also held once a month meeting in Lancaster, CA as part of our Warriors for Christ movement. We did this consistently for 4 years.

Nationwide ministries: I worked in conjunction with the Congressional Prayer Conference of Washington D.C.; worked in conjunction with the Gathering Place, a church for hard-core and punk rockers in Spokane, Washington; traveled and ministered with a prophetic ministry to churches in Washington, Minnesota, Louisiana, Nevada, New York, Maryland, Massachusetts, Pennsylvania, Washington D.C., Texas, Indiana, and Wisconsin; and I also was trained as a La Red field representative in 2007.

Our Spokane, WA meetings were a very high and very low time emotionally for me. We had some of our funniest of times ministering to the youth there. Our meetings in Spokane were very high energy, mosh pit, hardcore music style. We danced so hard at one point that we broke the stage and cracked the floor below us. The lowest for me because this is where I was when I heard about my father's passing. Leading while bleeding took me a step higher every time.

Even though I went through hard times I always kept on going, I kept moving, putting others needs before my own.

In Minnesota, there was a strong religious presence. They did not like that we prophesied over the kids, they asked that we pray over them instead, even though the words we spoke came to pass in many of their lives. At one meeting, the worship service was so beautiful everyone was singing in one accord; the church leadership was lined up against the wall in the back of the room. Then the most amazing thing happened. The youth turned to their parents and began to sing to them. A few even had prophecies for their parents. The whole dynamic changed from the judgmental attitudes about our meetings from there on in. God in his infinite wisdom always had a way of protecting us. He would "flip the script" in our favor every time. In Louisiana, we had amazing moments also. Some good, some bad. Picture this: A black Pastor with a multiethnic team traveling with him. We were invited but not welcomed by all. We were notified of this by the three bullets left on the doorstep where we were staying. But the kids loved us! The younger kids would imitate Dr. Rivers while playing; I want to be Dr. Rivers! Grabbing the invisible microphone out of the other kids' hands. At one of our evening meetings another miracle happened.

Here we are in an Urban Community and a busload of kids walk in from a neighboring white community church. They joined hands and put their arms around each other as they walked to the altar, praying, and crying together. It was the most beautiful thing I have ever seen. In a city where there are deep roots of racism, there was unity like never before. The next generation caught it here and are making the change. This is also one of the weirdest places we have had a meeting. The church sanctuary was converted from a mortuary, the cremation oven was still in the wall. Talk about having life and death in the same room. Unbelievable.

Many of the people and organizations that I have worked with over the years I'm still in contact with and have great relationships with. I have proven over the years that *faithfulness* and *consistency* are key components in serving others; this is what God looks for in His servants. I have always kept moving forward helping others no matter what the cost, this is what has led to my recognition and promotions. Not only did I gain experience through the years, but I *also* gained credibility and promotions. Since I have been loyal over little God has made me ruler over much! As of today, one of the main components of my work with iChange Nations is *Bringing Back the Lost Art of Honor* with the Golden Rule.

Do you know what I mean by the Golden Rule? You would be surprised to know that many people today don't know. The Golden Rule is the principle of treating others as you want to be treated. It is a maxim that is found in many religions and cultures around the world. It can be considered an *ethic of reciprocity* in some religions, although different religions treat it differently. The philosophy of the Golden Rule has been in our history from 1,000,000 BC until today. Every religion has a verse in their biblical scriptures that talks about the principles of the Golden Rule. It is a universal language. It is a law written on the human heart. The law of God.

Dale Carnegie's *How to Win Friends and Influence People*, a self-help book that sold 15 million copies, is based on the *Golden Rule* and says it best, "Philosophers have been speculating on the rules of human relationships for thousands of years, and there has evolved only one important precept. Zoroaster taught it to his followers in Persia twenty-five hundred years ago. Confucius preached it in China. Lao-tse, the founder of Taoism, taught it to his disciples. Buddha preached it on the bank of the Ganges. The sacred books of Hinduism taught it a thousand years before that. Jesus summed it up in one thought, probably the most important rule in the world: *Do unto others as you would have others do unto you*" (page number needed).

Everyone wants to feel that they are important in their little world. They don't want to listen to cheap, insincere flattery, but crave sincere appreciation. All of us want that. We long to be recognized and noticed by others. To feel that human connection with others. That is why this time when the whole world is in isolation due to the Coronavirus is so difficult. It is amazing to watch how people are coming up with new and creative ways to still interact with each other online. Talk shows and movie stars are having group chats. Musicians are playing and creating from their home studios. I caught a video of Andrew Lloyd Webber playing songs by request on his piano today, something I wouldn't normally listen to, but it was very soothing and enjoyable. This is a great time for everyone to just slow down, enjoy this time with our families. I look at this as a time to "reset" our lives. Reset your priorities.

Look around you and how you live your daily lives. Have you done all that you can do to serve others? If not, let's *activate* now the Golden Rule, and "do unto others what you would have others do unto you" in your everyday lives.

Let me share how the Golden Rule ties in with what I have done over the years in serving others,

In 2006 a man named Mussie Hailu, an Interfaith Golden-Rule activist from Ethiopia, translated McKenna's interfaith golden-rule poster into African languages and distributed *fifty thousand* copies, including one to every African head of state. He has also traveled extensively to most parts of the world promoting the universal peace prayer "May Peace Prevail on Earth" and addressing the issue of the culture of peace, reconciliation, right human relationship, interfaith harmony, the eradication of poverty, environmental protection and

reverence for life. He strongly emphasizes the need of **being the** *"change we want to see in the world"* and to follow the pathway to peace which leads us from darkness to light, from despair to hope, from killing each other to co-existence, from war to peace, from hate to love, from holding grudges to forgiveness, and from competition to cooperation, and that practicing the Golden Rule on a daily basis can lead to a better world.

In 2010 had the United Nations adopt April 5 as International Golden Rule Day. Hailu promoted the Golden Rule with the UN, the United Religions Initiative (http://www.uri.org), and many other organizations. This is where our paths crossed, and our visions and work became one. Dr. Rivers met Mussie Hailu in Kenya in 2010. As Dr. Rivers was meeting with one of the heads of state mentioned above. After this meeting I began closely working with Mussie Hailu in the quest of obtaining Golden Rule proclamations around the world. As of today, IChange Nations has now honored and appointed Golden Rule Ambassadors around the globe in 180 nations. In 2017 we created an IChange Nations award in Mussie Hailu's name in honor of his work.

On Saturday, August 19, 2017 the press release read: "Ambassador Dr. Clyde Rivers, Founder and President of iChange Nations™ has approved a new award in honor of a Top World Peace Activist and Philanthropist, Ambassador Mussie Hailu. This award is the iChange Nations™ Ambassador Mussie Hailu Global Peace Award. Ambassador Hailu is known worldwide to be a man of high values, deep care for humanity, and works around the world with the message of the Golden Rule."

The "Ambassador Mussie Hailu Global Peace Award," is an iChange Nations™ Award intended to acknowledge, recognize and appreciate the efforts of individuals or organizations throughout the world who are committed to promoting a culture of peace, compassion, human dignity, and the teaching of the Golden Rule with mutual respect and co-existence among followers of different religions and cultures.

Ambassador Mussie Hailu is working at regional, national and international levels. His efforts involve promoting peace, reconciliation, interfaith harmony, and world citizenship. In addition, he labors to protect human rights, enhancing respect and human dignity and compassion for all forms of life around the world. He also actively works against the proliferation of small arms and light weapons promoting disarmament. His efforts are also directed at constructive dialogue, building bridges for international cooperation, and promoting the teaching of the Golden Rule as a guiding principle. Ambassador Clyde Rivers further stated, "Ambassador Mussie

Hailu is one of the most influential men I know around the world impacting humanity for good. It is a great honor for my organization, iChange Nations™, to be able to create an award in his honor. Anyone receiving this award will be an example of what our world so desperately needs. True global peace representatives honoring mankind by living the Golden Rule, treating others the way they want to be treated." This also promotes the *be the change you want to see in the world.*

iChange Nations™ is the World's largest honoring network establishing cultures of honor in the World. We are proud to now have the "Ambassador Mussie Hailu Global Peace

Award" with which to honor qualified people changing the world.

Even though this section seems to tell the story of Mussie Hailu and Dr. Clyde Rivers, it also speaks to my work and service to every person that has been recognized and honored with the Golden Rule Award through iChange Nations. I was the person serving the people behind the scenes through my work in administration to make these awards and to coordinate all the details surrounding the events to honor the people throughout the world.

I Change Nations started out as an idea. An idea that was from God. *Bring Back the Lost Art of Honor.* Who really *looks* to honor others? The bible says give, and it shall be given back to you! So, what started out as honoring 30 people in Grand, Rapids Michigan (our first Golden Rule Honor event after meeting Mussie Hailu) is now a worldwide organization.

I believe this is what is missing in the world today, *New Business Leadership models* are needed. As part of iChange Nations we also help build other people's business initiatives around the world. This gift of leadership is visionary, a forward-looking gift that enables people to stay focused on where God might be leading them as individuals, businesses, congregations, and communities at any given time. These leaders look more to where they are going rather than where they currently are, or where they have been. Good leaders motivate others to work together in ways that help them *achieve more together* than any could on their own. Good leaders provide examples of how we should order our lives to honor and glorify God and those around us.

*Servant leadership* is a leadership philosophy in which the main goal of the leader is to serve. This is different from traditional leadership where the leader's focus is on the thriving of their company or organization. A servant leader shares power and puts the needs of the employees first; this helps people develop and perform as highly efficient as possible. Servant leadership inverts the norm, which puts the customer service associates as a main priority. Instead of the people working to serve the leader, *the leader exists to serve the people.* Some great examples of this in our history are Martin Luther King Jr., Nelson Mandela, Mahatma Gandhi, Mother Teresa, and Albert Schweitzer; they are some of the world's greatest leaders in humanity. Martin Luther King Jr. did not always want to be a leader of the Civil Rights movement in the U.S., but he knew that there was a need for equality in the world. Nelson Mandela fought against apartheid, a system of racial segregation. In his lifetime of service to the people he had his share of highs and lows. From winning a very controversial election to becoming the 1st President of South Africa, to then serving a life sentence in prison. He was released after serving 27 years and after his release continued to be an activist on social justice. After serving 27 years in prison he was not bitter. He continued to serve the people to the best of his ability. His life is another great example of how serving others is rewarded. Nelson Mandela went on to receive more than 250 honors including the Nobel Peace Prize.

# Chapter 6

## Royalty Over Much

Joseph's Story in the Bible is a good example of how God can take you to the top. Although Joseph came from a dysfunctional family of constant infighting, emotional manipulation, and conniving undercurrents, he was destined to become a great leader. In Genesis 37, his story begins with a lofty dream at the age of seventeen; Joseph was a dreamer his older brothers despised. They already deeply resented Joseph because he was clearly their father's favorite child, but after Joseph revealed to his brothers a dream in which they would bow down to him, it was just the beginning of the story for the young visionary. One day, while out in the fields, they saw Joseph coming and conspired against him. "Here comes the dreamer," they said to one another. "Let us kill him and we will see what will become of his dreams." But instead, they seized him and sold him into slavery. Betrayed by his family, he was taken away by a caravan of slave traders who took him to Egypt where he served in the house of a powerful leader named Potiphar. Seemingly overnight, Joseph's ambitious dream had turned into a horrible nightmare. Though his life situation had taken a drastic turn for the worse, and he found himself a slave in a distant land, in all the turmoil that surrounded him Joseph learned and held onto the belief that nothing can ever separate us from the love of God; no unfavourable shift in circumstances, geography, or social status could thwart God's favourable purposes in Joseph's life. The Bible says that the Lord was with Joseph, and he became successful and prosperous in everything he touched. The young Hebrew slave remained faithful to the Lord in every situation and always maintained his integrity, and he found favour in the sight of the Lord and was made ruler over much.

In my life, I truly believe this is the same story for me. I started out life fighting to survive, but God has had his hand on me every step of the way. When my mother died, he was with me;

when my marriage failed, he was with me; when I thought about suicide and drank my problems away, he was there. I'm no worse or no better than anyone else. God just patiently loved me through it all until I turned to him for answers. I learned, just like Joseph did, to hold on to the belief that nothing can separate me from the love of God. I see now that God has been with me through it all and has rewarded me for my diligence and consistency. Consistency is a very important key in one's life to be successful in anything. Being consistent in your work builds good habits and helps in the moving forward of your dreams. If you are all over the board trying this and trying that it is harder to get anywhere. That is why I said that it is important to find your passion or what you enjoy doing in life, because then you have a vision for the future.

Consistency has played a great part in the rewards of my service. I have been very consistent in my life. I have lived in the same house for 35 years, where I raised my 2 boys and worked with Dr. Rivers for 25 years. I also worked in retail 15 years before going to Miracle Faith Church. This fact has allowed people to see that we are always there for them and they know where they can find us if they need anything. God has seen our consistency and faithfulness and we know this by what he has given us. We started teaching in one school, now we have ongoing work with 4 schools, and one is named after Dr. Rivers, the Dr. Rivers School of Skills and Acquisitions in

Nigeria. We started to honour people with the Golden Rule, which turned into the largest honour system in the world when God gave Dr. Rivers the idea for iChange Nations. Dr. Rivers has been promoted from a Pastor to Prophet, Teacher, Ambassador, Knight, Chief, Don, all while remaining true to our beginning roots of the church. At the beginning of working with Dr. Rivers, I, too, thought he was a dreamer. He would always talk about changing the world.

At some of our early meetings – we would meet every Monday night, me, Betty, and Dr. Rivers – we were planning for the great future even when we had nothing at the time. We could not even buy 1 soda between the three of us because we didn't have enough money. I have been there with Dr. Rivers all along the way and have seen it all. From not having a car to having cars given to us. From me getting 3- day pay or quits on my home and almost losing it more than a few times, to having someone pay it off. Through it all we keep moving forward no matter what. So now; I begin to step out Internationally. Still in awe that this small-town girl is going on her first International trip to Uganda. Here are some other examples of my International work and service to others over the years:

Overseer of Global Executive Leadership (UACCMI) United Association of Christian Churches and Ministers International. Executive Director, North America Division of IPI-Interfaith Peace-Building Initiative Addis Ababa, Ethiopia. Board Member of iChange Nations and Executive Director of Administration. International Ambassador for the Golden Rule.

Special Projects Coordinator to Amb. Clyde Rivers for Burundi, Africa. Assisted in the Administration of outreach ministries and serving the people in Uganda, Kenya, Nigeria, Ivory Coast, and South Africa. Executive Director of Operations of Latin University of Theology USA/Africa English Extensions. International Overseer of the Administration, of United Graduate College and Seminary. Established and maintained an International Internet Radio

Station "Open My Ears for Christ.com" You see it has been a lot of hard work, but it has been an enjoyable work, not feeling like work at all, because I know it is my passion and my call, and I know God is with me. I have now had the opportunity to travel to Uganda, Kenya, Nigeria, Dubai, Guatemala, Guyana, and the UK and I'm just getting started.

I look forward to the day when I hear him say, "Well done, good and faithful servant. You have been faithful over a little; I will set you as a ruler over much. Enter into the joy of your master" (Matthew 25:23).

Although most read this verse as something we obtain in Heaven, we can have this all here and now! God has called us to pray: "Our Kingdom come, thy will be done, on Earth as it is in Heaven." We can live this prayer out now. We can have all the promises of God here and now, on this earth if we believe that we can.

## THINK BOOK 💡

Can you think of a time when your actions turned into a great reward?

_____

_____

_____

_____

_____

_____

_____

_____

# Chapter 7

## Know Your Limits

In serving others it is very important to know your limits. Never do more than where your heart leads you. This is the time when knowing the difference between the gifted and the called comes into play. As I stated earlier, all can serve but not all are gifted. Knowing your limits is very important. People that are not necessarily gifted to serve can commit to too much too fast and at the start they are so willing to help another person that they cannot break the *routine of things* they have set later. *Consistency can also build bad habits.* It is important here to learn to let your *yes be yes* and *your no be no*. Here is where the servant trait of discernment will help greatly. It will help to weed out those who really need help and are thankful for it and discern those who are just seeking to always take from others.

Jesus knew his limits; when Jesus heard about John's execution; he withdrew to be alone. John was Jesus's cousin and the only one that seemed to understand his mission. Now John is gone. Jesus wants some quiet time to grieve and gain perspective. But does he get it? No. When the multitudes heard of his presence, the people sought him out, thinking only of their own needs. This is the true act of service and sacrifice. Jesus would have been justified in saying, "Can't you all see that I need some time away from all of you?" But he didn't; instead he responded by focusing on the needs of others. He still had compassion for the crowds of people; even amidst his own problems he began to serve and heal their sick. The example to be learned here: *One of the greatest remedies for our own suffering is serving others.* Servanthood and serving becomes the solution for both the serving and the one being served. God will sometimes use others to help you. In serving others we will learn who we are.

In this time of the Coronavirus Social Distancing, we are locked down to our homes or as I like to call it, "Protective Custody." Schools are closed, all businesses are closed, unless they are *essential* to life such as grocery stores, pharmacies, automotive repair and gas stations. It is difficult to serve others when the world has literally shut down, but people are finding new and creative ways of serving others. No touch food pantries, drive-in church services, car processions for birthday parties, all the online activities of people serving others with their own unique gifting and talents. TV Stars and popular musicians are doing their "thing" online. What may have started as a thing to do out of boredom can turn into something else, they can really help someone that is alone and lonely. Music is something we all have in common and is very healing. As we have seen in Italy and now in New York, people are using music to stay connected with neighborhoods singing together from in front of their home or from their balconies. It's a beautiful thing to see. I talked earlier about how the world is only thinking about themselves and is stuck in the me, myself, and I mentality. We can see that during a "crisis" *Christ is* there, in the midst of us. The best in the hearts of God's people come to the surface. Why does it take a world-wide pandemic to make this change? And after all this sickness and chaos settles down will it have had a lasting effect on the world? Will we be kinder to one another on a daily basis, as we were in this pandemic, or will we revert to our old mindsets? This has been a beautiful time to watch how people are coming together for the good of another.

Anyway, getting back to knowing your limits, how to help others and not lose yourself is very important. Seeking time to be alone is a good thing. It helps us to refocus on what is important. In the business of life, we can tend to get off track with our vision. When we are alone, we can hear more clearly what God is speaking to us pertaining to what and where we should be going. Being alone helps us prepare and energize ourselves for the next task at hand.

Set priorities and set your boundaries – you don't have to answer your phone every time it rings, just check your messages often; if someone doesn't leave a message, I look at it as if it was not that important to the other person either. Set your boundaries; as you feel overwhelmed and need some space, setting boundaries helps to maintain a healthy balanced relationship. When I'm feeling overwhelmed in my service to others, I like to change up my routine or change my environment. Changing my routine breaks up the monotony. Getting away to a different environment helps to reenergize me. I was able to recently drive to Vegas for a mini vacation; I spent three days just for me. I went to see one of Celine Dion's last shows in Vegas and just had a lot of good rest and refocus time.

Overall, making others great through service makes us happy; there are enough proven health benefits that there is something to be said for helping others. When you are helping others, you will often feel better about yourself, increasing the likelihood that your next experience will be a positive one rather than a negative one.

Knowing your call and setting priorities will also help to set your limits. I know I'm just called to serve behind the scenes, I know my call. Like I said earlier I'm not one that has looked to be up front to speak to others; I have preached sermons, but I know that is not my strength. A story of how I know my call, that I can share: On one of my International trips I led a team of people into a foreign country by myself; boy, was this a learning experience. I was asked twice to do things that I was not there to do. This was why we had put together this particular team. We each had our own roles, giftings, and assignments to do. After being asked repeatably to do things I was not called to do and then being put on the spot publicly, I stood my ground. After being introduced to a crowd of thousands I said a few words introducing my team and why we were there and politely handed the microphone over to my colleague on stage. The message was received. I was not asked again to do anything that was designed to use me to promote their own agendas and I was able to remain in my call. In the Bible there is a great story of knowing your call and setting your priorities. Notice the exchange between Jesus and Martha: "Martha had a sister called Mary, who also sat at Jesus' feet and heard His word. But Martha was distracted with much serving, and she approached Him and said, 'Lord, do You not care that my sister has left me to serve alone? Therefore, tell her to help me.' And Jesus answered and said to her, 'Martha, Martha, you are worried and troubled about many things. But one thing is needed, and Mary has chosen *that good part*, which will not be taken from her" (Luke 10:39-42).

Scripture doesn't record whether Jesus' response made a lasting impression on Martha's understanding, but we can hope this spiritual lesson is so inseparably linked to our priorities and how it will favorably impact us. What did Mary have that Martha needed? What was the "good part" Mary chose? In a world filled with distractions, the story of Mary and Martha can help you set your life in order. To set your priorities. What is important to you? The many things Martha was troubled about were needless, while the one thing she neglected was needful and necessary. Martha's care and work were good in their proper season and place. And you can see that when she was over-extended in her serving, she became jealous of Mary and frustrated.

*Never let service to others take you beyond*

*your life values.*

*Dr. Robin A. Lococo*

# Chapter 8

## You Never Know Who's Watching

You never know whose watching and you never know whose life you might be changing for the better. Remember your service will be noticed. We don't always realize how at the time, but it is. Working with Dr. Rivers over the years we have honored thousands of people with the Golden Rule Ambassador Awards. We have looked to honor individuals who have accomplished great things in the world and have made a difference to humanity. We always served to the best of our ability. Because we have recognized others it has come back to us. Recognition and service to others will be noticed. Honoring and serving others bring rewards, usually when you least expect it and from the strangest of places and people.

Here's the story of how I received the Presidential Award:

A certain man had been watching my work with Dr. Rivers and he had noticed me. It just happened that on the same day and same time he was praying and asking God who to honor, while researching me online and seeing what I had done throughout the years, I texted him. I had never interacted with this man before until this time. So, when I texted him at this same time, he considered it a sign that I was the one God wanted him to honor. I had no idea he was even considering me for this award. Months had gone by and one day Dr. Rivers calls me and says he has something for me. My presidential award had been shipped to Dr. Rivers address for him to give it to me. This may seem unusual to some, but this shows how God can use anything and anybody to get your rewards to you. I was shocked to learn of receiving this honor. I had no idea this was happening. But, like I said, you never know who's watching!

In Mathew 6, Jesus confronts our tendency of wanting to practice good deeds before other people in order to be seen by them. Some may read this book and think that I am being boastful in flaunting my awards. But that is not my intention at all in writing this book. I know that I am no better than anyone else. It is by the grace of God that I have had the opportunities that I have had. I am humbled by the fact that God has been with me every step along the way. I am thankful for all the great people that I have met and had the opportunity to work with and to serve. I want to thank Point of Grace for even considering me for the Donald J. Trump Presidential Award, it is such an honor to be recognized for my work.

I would also like to thank Congressman Danny K. Davis for my Top 20 Woman of the Year Woman's Day Award and give recognition to all the hard work that went into that beautiful event. It was an honor to sit among such great humanitarians. Last, but not least, my first award for my organization

Challenged Champions and Heroes Special Needs Icon of the Year Award.

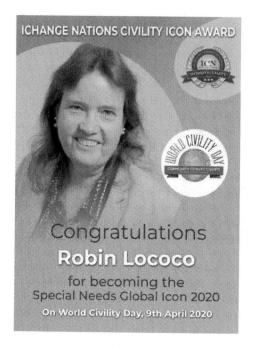

My nomination was approved by the World Civility Counsel and I was humbled to be a part of a class of people such as the Former President of Malawi Joyce Banda.

My point in writing this book is to encourage others to *live life intentionally*. To step out and try new things; that small steps can lead to big things. There are so many people hurting in the world today. Reach out and make a change in someone's life.

Don't wait to find a starting place – start now! You can't take material goods with you when you die, they say the richest place in the world is in the graveyard, how many people have died not fulfilling their destiny. Why not enjoy life here on earth? Live your legacy now by your actions while you're still alive. Live your life to the fullest. Think about how we affect each other's lives in a positive way. Think about the person that may have been created to find the cure for the Coronavirus, and he may have died from a drug overdose. If he had lived, how much different his life and the lives of thousands of others would have been.

*There is no greater agony than bearing an*

*untold story inside you.*

*Maya Angelou*

# Chapter 9

## Unintentional Legacy

Living life intentionally brings an unintentional legacy. At least that is how it happened for me. I was just going about my life with what I believed God had for me to do in life. Like I said at the beginning, I wasn't looking for this to happen, but it did. My obedience, faithfulness, and strength in my commitment to walk out every assignment every day made this happen. Leaving a life legacy is not about running the race fast, but effectively. Your pain and what you go through is shaping your legacy whether you realize it or not.

THINK BOOK 💡

What do you think people will people say about you?

_____

_____

_____

_____

_____

_____

_____

As I received my Presidential Award, I was overwhelmed by the comments from my friends, family and work associates. It really got me thinking about how my life has affected others for the good and bad. It caused me to think a little deeper on my legacy and what I will be leaving behind.

These are some of the comments that were left on my FB wall:

So, deserving. /One of excellency and faith./ Your dedication to excellence and worship of the Almighty God, has brought you well deserved honor. /I am very thankful for you. Well done my friend./ Awesome work Robin you're beautiful. Wow! Congratulations many blessings to you woman of God. /Awesome job!/ Well-deserved honor to a hard-working servant. /You're the best xxx-ooo./ They say the dynamite comes in small packages well you are awesome and amazing and a whole lot of dynamite. You are awesome. /One of the best. Keep up the hard work. You deserve it, hard work pays off. /You do so much and deserve this and so much more you're a great person who loves the Lord and is always trying to help others and so faithful in all that you do, I am thankful to know you. /You are one of the sweetest people I know always loving and kind. Continue to let God use you mightily./ Greeting in Jesus name. I am so glad on your offering for the work of God Kingdom plan in Pakistan. I will be so happy If you lead me for better work of God's Kingdom work in Pakistan. I thank you for your support and your kind leading will be strength in here. /Well done. Great job! /A great voice for humanity. /Thank you for the all the efforts, hours spent, and sacrifice to benefit mankind. Much favor to you, God's princess. /We give you the honor because you have earned it. Dr. Lococo, thank you for...being the most incredible teacher/advisor/motivator/role model/and friend all in one. Thank you for your patience, your passion about your work, your sense of humor in and out of the classroom. Pushing me to do my best work. Making class fun to go to truly being the best teacher I have ever had. Getting me so involved with the psych department. Thank you for your unconditional support. Your quick wit. Making me intrinsically want to learn, getting me interested in things I never thought I would like originally. Putting up with me in general. Getting me excited about Christian Leadership and learning in general! Being involved with everything at United Graduate College and Seminary International but still always making yourself available to me. /Modeling good leadership, thank you for being part of my life!

These comments show you how service is recognized by others!

I kept these comments not to boast about myself, but to look back upon them when times are rough. In the days of adversity, they encourage me to keep moving. Especially at those times when I feel like I'm not doing enough, and we all go through those times.

I now have walked you through my path in life: of *loyalty over little* to…. *royalty over much.* I want you to know I still get hit with some of the same mind battles I did at the very beginning of my journey. This is a very normal process in life. I just have a better understanding of how to see the thoughts coming and deal with them a lot quicker and better now. I like to call it the "Perfect Storm" when the thoughts in your head, conveniently line up with what you're seeing and hearing around you and try to strengthen the negativity around you. It's just a smokescreen. The enemy has no power over you. He only has the power that *you give* him. So, do all to stand.

When we reach the pearly gates, what if the *first* question we are asked is, "How many people did you help?"

As you finish this book,

## THINK BOOK 💡

Has your personal philosophy on serving changed? And how?

_____

_____

_____

_____

_____

_____

_____

_____

_____

## THINK BOOK 💡

Give 2 examples of how you have served others, and how did they respond?

_____

_____

_____

_____

_____

_____

_____

_____

_____

_____

*Carve your name on hearts, not tombstones.*

*A legacy is etched into the minds of others*

*and the stories they share about you*

*Shannon Adler*

Dr. Robin A. Lococo with Albert Nassagare Presidents
Protocol of Burundi

Dr. Robin A. Lococo with the Queen Mother of Torro

Dr. Robin A. Lococo with the King of Torro

Dr. Lococo receiving the Universal Peace Ambassador Award

Dr. Robin A. Lococo with Former Amb. of Guatamala
Floridalma Franco

Dr. Robin A. Lococo receiving the Top 20 Congressional
Woman's Day Award

Dr. Robin A. Lococo receiving the ICN Global Leadership
Award

Dr. Robin A. Lococo with Amb. of Suriname Henry McDonald

H.E. De Wheno Aholu Menu Toyi .The Akran of the
Badgry Kingdom

Dr. Robin A. Lococo with Former President of Nigeria
Olesgun Obassanjo

CCH Penny Heflebower, Denise Moraga and Dr. Robin A. Lococo at Camp Kangaroo

Dr. Robin Lococo at the U.S. Capitol in Washington, D.C.

Manufactured by Amazon.ca
Bolton, ON

13816805R00069